Top 100 Tips for Windows 8

By Tim Sievers

Website: www.tims-tips.com

Email: tim@tims-tips.com

Table of Contents

Introduction

Hello, I'm Tim Sievers. I've used every Microsoft Operating System (OS) since the days of MS-DOS in the 1980's and over the years I've seen huge improvements in usability and design. However, looking back only one previous version of the OS stands out in my mind as a truly radical re-think of its predecessors, until now. In its day, Windows 95 was a game changer, users no longer had to deal with the dreaded DOS command-line because the user-friendly graphical Desktop was at the forefront of the user experience.

After 17 years, Microsoft has dared to re-imagine Windows again. The promotion of the new "Modern User Interface" (Modern UI) ahead of the Desktop and Microsoft's push for developers to focus on building web-based touch-enabled apps for a new generation of tablets, laptops and PC's is a major change. I can still see the Desktop remaining a big part of the user experience for a long time to come, but like Windows 95 all those years ago, Windows 8 stands out as a radical redesign.

Recently updated for Windows 8.1, this guide is a collection of the best 100 tips that I have found for Windows 8. Designed to help you get up to speed quickly, this guide covers both the new Modern UI and the improved features of the Desktop. Because Windows 8 is built for both touchscreen and traditional computing devices I have included both touchscreen gesture and keyboard/mouse instructions. For many tips, the touch gesture instructions use a separate heading called "**Touch**" and the keyboard/mouse instructions use the heading "**Key/Mouse**".

Also, as a bonus extra, I have included a list of the most common Windows 8 Keyboard Shortcuts. This handy reference is divided into several categories to help you quickly find the shortcut you need, when you need it. So, whether you've just started using Windows 8 or you've been using it for a while, I'm sure you'll find some useful tips here that will improve your Windows 8 experience.

Now, lets get started!

Chapter 1 – Getting Started

When you first use Windows 8 the most obvious change you will notice is the new Start Menu (now called the Start Screen), which automatically appears as you start Windows, and takes up the whole display. At first this sweeping change of design, called the Modern UI, can be a bit of a shock for even the most experienced Windows user. Some common responses upon first seeing Windows 8 are "Oh My God! Where's the Desktop?" "What happen to the Start menu?" or "How do I find my way around this thing?"

If you're feeling a bit lost too, don't worry, in this chapter you'll learn how to navigate the new Windows 8 environment using either touch gestures or keyboard and mouse shortcuts.

This chapter also includes some of the best new features found in Windows 8.1.

Tip # 1 – Window Charms

A menu bar of commonly used system commands, called "charms", can be accessed from the right side of your screen. These charms include a handy shortcut back to the Start Screen as well as Search, Share, Devices and Settings. You can access the Charms menu in the following ways:

Touch – Swipe inwards from the right edge of the screen.

Key/Mouse – Move the mouse pointer to the upper or lower right corners of the screen, then move the mouse along the right-hand edge of the screen towards the charms as they appear.

Note: Many of the keyboard shortcuts used in Windows 8 involve a special key on your keyboard called the Windows Logo Key. On an existing keyboard it should look like this ⊞ or on a new keyboard like this ⊞ and is located in the bottom left-hand corner between the **Ctrl** and **Alt** keys. Throughout this guide I will use the new Windows 8 logo ⊞ to refer to this key. For example, the Charms menu can also be accessed via a keyboard shortcut, by pressing the Windows Logo Key and the letter "C" key at the same time. This shortcut can be showed as: ⊞ + **C**

Tip # 2 – Quick Launch

Have you been wondering why Microsoft removed the traditional Start menu or how to find your apps, settings and files in Windows 8? The answers can be found in the evolution of desktop searching. The speed and functionality of Search Tools have improved so much in recent years that one of the quickest ways to find and launch a file or app, is to search for it. So instead of *searching* for the Start menu, you should *start* with the Search charm.

Touch – Swipe inwards from the right edge of the screen to bring up the Charms menu. Then tap on the Search charm. You can filter your results by tapping on the dropdown list and selecting a search category, like Settings or Files.

Key/Mouse – Go to the Start Screen and just start typing to bring up the Search charm. You can filter your results by clicking on the dropdown list and selecting a search category, like Settings or Files.

Note: You can also use the following keyboard shortcuts to jump directly to popular search options. To search Everywhere use:  + **Q**. To search for Settings use: + **W**. To search for Files use: + **F**.

Tip # 3 – Quick Cycle

To quickly cycle between open apps:

Touch – Swipe inwards from the left edge of the screen.

Key/Mouse – Move the mouse pointer into the upper left-hand corner and click to cycle through each app. You can also cycle through open apps with the keyboard shortcut: **Alt + Tab**

Tip # 4 – Show Recent Apps

To show a list of your recently used apps:

Touch – Swipe in and back out from the left edge of the screen.

Key/Mouse – Move the mouse pointer to the upper or lower left corners of the screen, then move the mouse along the left-hand edge of the screen towards the center. You can also use the keyboard shortcut: ■ + **Tab**. Hold down the ■ key and keep tapping the **Tab** key to cycle through the list.

Tip # 5 – App bars

To keep the look of the Modern UI in Windows 8 crisp & clean, many app commands have been hidden from view in menu bars that, depending on the app you're using, can be called into view from the top and/or bottom of the screen. To show these app command bars:

Touch – Perform a small swipe inwards from the bottom or top edge of the screen.

Key/Mouse – **Right-click** in open space to see the app command bars. Or use the shortcut: ⊞ + Z

Tip # 6 – Selecting an Item and Finding Greater Context

In Windows 8, you can select individual items on the screen to show more details and in many cases, reveal additional commands via App bars and Context Menus.

Touch – You can select an item by performing a touch-screen gesture called a "Long-Press". To perform a **Long-Press**, tap & hold your finger on the screen for a few seconds, then release it. In the Modern UI, a tick will appear on the top right corner of the item. In the Desktop, a square will appear underneath your finger before you release it from the screen.

Key/Mouse – **Right-click** on an item to select it and see more details.

Tip # 7 – Pin-Ups

In addition to using the Search charm to launch apps, you can "Pin" your favorite apps and file locations to the Start Screen for easy access.

Touch – To "Pin" an app to the Start Screen, locate the app with the Search charm and **long-press** on the search result to bring up the App command bar, then select **Pin to Start**.

To "Pin" a File Location to the Start Screen, locate a file with the Search charm and **long-press** on the search result to bring up the App command bar, then select **Open file location**. **Long-press** on the File Location to bring up the context menu, then select **Pin to Start**.

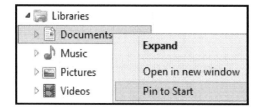

Key/Mouse – To "Pin" an app to the Start Screen, locate the app with the Search charm and **right-click** on the search result to bring up the App command bar, then select **Pin to Start**.

To "Pin" a File Location to the Start Screen, locate a file with the Search charm and **right-click** on the search result to bring up the App command bar, then select **Open file location**. **Right-click** on the File Location to bring up the context menu, then select **Pin to Start**.

Tip # 8 – Closing Down

Wondering where the "Close" button is for your Modern UI apps? Well, it simply doesn't exist anymore! Instead to close an app just:

Touch – Swipe your finger down from the top of the screen to the bottom of the screen.

Key/Mouse – Click and drag downwards on the app from the top of the screen to the bottom of the screen. Or use the keyboard shortcut: **⊞ + . + Down Arrow**

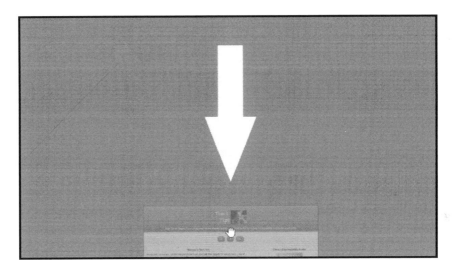

Tip # 9 – Moving Sideways

Unlike traditional websites or Desktop apps, many Modern UI apps in Windows 8 are designed for panning or scrolling sideways.

Touch – Simply swipe or slide your finger left or right to pan across the screen.

Key/Mouse – Hmmm horizontal scrolling with a traditional mouse, sounds painful right? Don't worry, you don't have to try and use the awkward scroll bar at the bottom of the screen, instead you can use the mouse wheel to quickly scroll sideways. Scroll down to go to the right and scroll up to go left.

Tip # 10 – Semantic Zoom

Semantic Zoom allows you to see a high-level zoomed-out view within many Modern UI lists, apps and on the Start Screen. This zoomed-out view let's you see the over all structure so you can quickly navigate and browse through content.

Touch – Pinch two fingers together on the screen to zoom out, then tap to go to a different section.

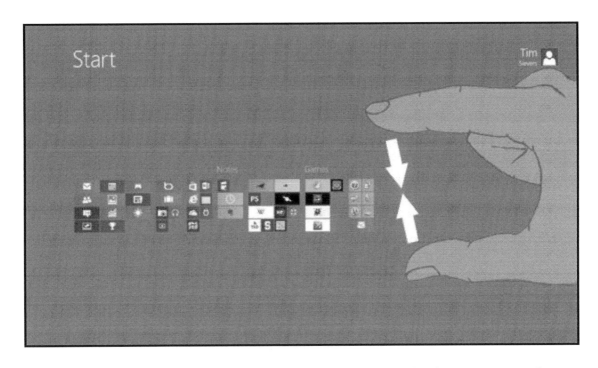

Key/Mouse – Hold the **Ctrl** key while using the mouse wheel to zoom out, then click to go to a different section. You can also use, **Ctrl + Shift + the minus sign (-)** to zoom out and **Ctrl + Shift + "+"** to zoom in.

Tip # 11 – Appy Snaps

If you like to work with more than one app at a time, you can easily snap Modern UI apps to either side of the screen for multitasking.

Touch – Begin by swiping your finger down from the top of the screen as if you were going to close the app, but pause when the app window shrinks on the screen, then slide your finger to the side of the screen until a vertical dividing line appears and release your finger. Now open a second app and it will snap into the spare space on the screen. You can tap and drag the dividing line to show more of one app than the other.

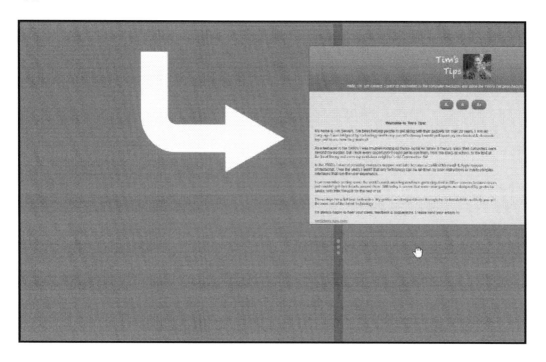

Key/Mouse – You can snap an app and cycle through snap positions by pressing the Windows Logo Key with the Period button and the Left or Right Arrow keys:

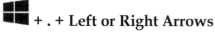 **+ . + Left or Right Arrows**

Then open a second app and it will snap into the spare space on the screen. You can also click and drag the dividing line to show more of one app than the other.

Tip # 12 – The Return of the Start Button

The Windows 8.1 update brings a Start button back to the Desktop and also to the Start Screen. However, unlike the Start button in previous versions of Windows, this Start button doesn't reveal the old fashion Start menu. Instead it is a quick shortcut between the Desktop and the Start Screen. It also hides a very handy tool called the Quick Link menu.

Touch – Simply tap on the **Start button** in the Desktop to show the Start Screen. In the Start Screen swipe in and back out from the left edge of the screen to reveal the Start button, then tap it to return to the Desktop. **Long-press** on the **Start button** to reveal the **Quick Link menu**.

Key/Mouse – Simply click on the **Start button** in the Desktop to show the Start Screen. In the Start Screen move the mouse to the bottom left-hand corner of the screen to reveal the Start button, then click on it to return to the Desktop. **Right-click** on the **Start button** to reveal the **Quick Link menu** or use: ⊞ + X

Tip # 13 – Launching to the Desktop

If you spend much of your time working in the Desktop then you'll love this! Windows 8.1 has a much requested new feature that makes your computer go directly to the Desktop when you sign in or close all apps on the screen.

Go to the Desktop and **long-press** or **right-click** on an empty area of the **Taskbar** to bring up the options menu, then tap or click **Properties**. Select the **Navigation** tab and select the checkbox next to **When I sign in or close all apps on a screen, go to the desktop instead of Start**. Then tap or click the **Apply** and **OK** buttons.

```
Start screen
☑ When I sign in or close all apps on a screen, go to the desktop
   instead of Start
```

Tip # 14 – Softening the Start Screen

For experienced Windows users, Windows 8 can take some getting use to, especially the jarring effect of switching from your favorite Desktop background to the bright full screen appearance of the Start Screen. Thankfully Microsoft has added a new feature in Windows 8.1 to soften the impact of this effect by allowing you to set your Desktop background to the Start Screen.

Go to the Desktop and **long-press** or **right-click** on an empty area of the **Taskbar** to bring up the options menu, then tap or click **Properties**. Select the **Navigation** tab and select the checkbox next to **Show my desktop background on Start**. Then tap or click the **Apply** and **OK** buttons.

Tip # 15 – Viewing Your Apps

In Windows 8.1 the Apps View, which displays a list of all your installed applications, is easier to access. To show the Apps View:

Touch – Simply swipe upwards on the Start Screen. Swipe downwards to go back to the Start Screen.

Key/Mouse – Click the down arrow icon that appears in the bottom left-hand corner below the Start Screen Tiles. Click the up arrow icon to go back to the Start Screen. Or use the shortcut: **Ctrl + Tab**

You can also adjust how the Apps View appears to make it work a bit like the old Start menu (especially when combined with the previous tip). Go to the Desktop and **long-press** or **right-click** on an empty area of the **Taskbar** to bring up the options menu, then tap or click **Properties**. Select the **Navigation** tab and select the Apps View options you prefer.

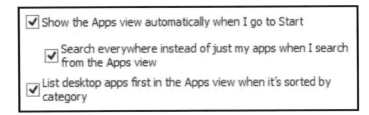

☑ Show the Apps view automatically when I go to Start

☑ Search everywhere instead of just my apps when I search from the Apps view

☑ List desktop apps first in the Apps view when it's sorted by category

Tip # 16 – Finding Some Peace & Quiet

Many of the apps in Windows 8 display notifications that make an alert sound to grab your attention 24/7. Windows 8.1 includes a new feature that lets you schedule some quiet time.

Touch – To adjust this feature, bring up the **Charms** menu, tap **Settings** and **Change PC settings**. Select **Search and apps**, then **Notifications** and scroll down to see the **Quiet hours** options. Then set your preferred times.

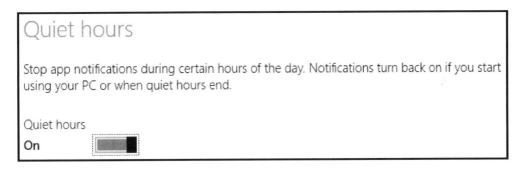

Quiet hours

Stop app notifications during certain hours of the day. Notifications turn back on if you start using your PC or when quiet hours end.

Quiet hours

On

Key/Mouse – To adjust this feature, press ⊞ + **I** to bring up **Settings** and click on **Change PC settings**. Select **Search and apps**, then **Notifications** and scroll down to see the **Quiet hours** options. Then set your preferred times.

Note: This tip only works when you're not using your Windows 8 device. For information on how to temporarily disable notifications when using Windows 8 see Tip # 27.

Tip # 17 – Connect To A Microsoft Account

Windows 8 gives you the choice to use either a Local user account or a Microsoft account. In the past most consumers would have used a Local account, but now the preferred option is a Microsoft account. With a Microsoft account you can download apps from the Windows Store, sync your PC settings across multiple devices and access Microsoft's SkyDrive cloud service. If you setup a Local account when you first configured Windows 8, you can easily switch it to a Microsoft account.

Bring up the **Charms** menu, select **Settings** and **Change PC Settings**. Then select **Accounts** and tap or click on the **Connect to a Microsoft account** button.

Tim

Local Account

Sign in with a Microsoft account to easily get your online email, photos, files and settings (like browser history and favorites) on all your devices.

Connect to a Microsoft account

You can sign in with an existing Microsoft account (including the following account types; @hotmail.com, @live.com or @outlook.com) or choose to create a new account.

Sign in to your Microsoft account

Sign in to easily get your online email, photos, files, and settings (like browser history and favorites) on all your devices. You can manage your synced settings at any time.

someone@example.com

Password

Don't have an account?

Create a new account

Privacy statement

Next   Cancel

Tip # 18 – Shutting Down

With no Start menu and no obvious Shutdown button, what's the best way to turn Windows 8 off? Actually Microsoft doesn't really want you to worry about shutting down your Windows 8 devices, with improved power management for older machines and a new feature called "Connected Standby" that allows newer machines to remain connected to the net 24/7 in sleep mode, shutting down seems so...last century! Right? No? Well ok, not everybody thinks that way, so here are the quickest ways to shutdown:

Touch – Bring up the **Charms** menu and select **Settings**, tap the **Power** button and select **Shut down**. You can also **long-press** on the **Start button** in the Desktop to access the **Quick Link menu**, then select **Shut down or sign out** and **Shut down.**

Key/Mouse – Press **Ctrl + Alt + Del** and click the **Power** button, then select **Shut down**. You can also **right-click** on the **Start button** to access the **Quick Link menu** (or use  + **X**), then select **Shut down or sign out** and **Shut down.**

Sleep

Shut down

Restart

Chapter 2 – Getting Personal

Microsoft's new Modern User Interface offers you a visually rich user environment. If you spend much of your time working in the Modern UI it will be important to get things looking the way you want. Customizing the User Interface can make your user experience more productive and enjoyable. In Windows 8 you can personalize your system with Lock Screen and Account pictures, change the color scheme and background tattoo images, add a printer and change your notification settings. You can also add, remove, resize, group and rearrange the live tiles that make up the Start Screen.

In this chapter you'll learn how to customize and improve the *look & feel* of the Modern UI.

Tip # 19 – Account Picture

The first place to start personalizing your computer is by changing your User Account Picture.

On the Start Screen, just tap or click on your Username in the top right-hand corner, then select **Change account picture**.

Of course, you can choose a picture from the Photos library but if your Windows 8 device has a camera you can take a snapshot or even better, choose **Video mode** to take a short 5-second video. Just tap or click anywhere on the screen to start recording and again to stop, then choose **OK** to select it.

Note: For best results when recording a video, stick to simple movements and facial expressions like turning to the camera and smiling!

Tip # 20 – Start Screen Color & Tattoos

Microsoft has included various different color schemes for you to choose from and so called "tattoos" that add stylish patterns to the Start Screen.

Bring up the **Charms** menu, select **Settings** and **Personalize**. Here you can mix and match color schemes and tattoos until you find the combination you like best.

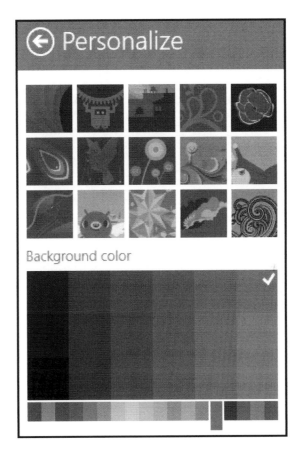

Tip # 21 – Lock Screen Picture

The Lock Screen is the first screen you see when you fire up Windows 8. You can choose from one of six specially design Lock Screen images, or use one of your own pictures to add a personal touch.

Bring up the **Charms** menu, select **Settings**, **Change PC Settings**, then choose **PC and devices**, **Lock screen**. Simply tap or click to choose a different image or select the **Browse** button to add your own picture.

Tip # 22 – Lock Screen Apps

In addition to showing you the date and time, the Lock Screen can show notifications and reminders for different apps.

Bring up the **Charms** menu, select **Settings**, **Change PC Settings**, then choose **PC and devices**, **Lock screen**. Scroll or swipe vertically on the right side of the screen to see the **Lock screen apps** settings. Simply tap or click a Plus 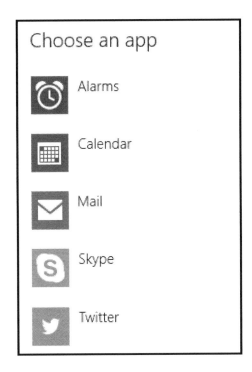 sign to add an app.

Choose an app

🕐 Alarms

📅 Calendar

✉ Mail

Ⓢ Skype

🐦 Twitter

Note: As well as the Alarms, Calendar, Mail, Skype and Weather apps, you can also add some third-party apps, like Twitter, which you can install for free from the Windows Store on the Start Screen.

Tip # 23 – Tile Size

The tiles pinned to your Start Screen can appear in four different sizes, as if to reflect their importance, but what's important to one person can be completely different to someone else. So Microsoft lets you change the size of the individual tiles to make your favorite tiles standout.

Long-press or right-click on a tile to bring up the App bar, then tap or click on the **Resize** button to adjust the tile size.

Tip # 24 – Removing Tiles

Tiles pinned to your Start Screen are best thought of as smart shortcuts that can display live data and notifications, but their still only shortcuts. So you can safely remove them without deleting any data or uninstalling any apps.

Long-press or right-click on a tile to bring up the App bar, and then tap or click on the **Unpin from Start** button to remove the tile.

Tip # 25 – Group & Arrange Tiles

You can rearrange the position of tiles on the Start Screen and create new groups of tiles.

Touch – To relocate a tile, long-press on the tile to select it, then move the tile to a new location and release your finger from the screen. To create a new group of tiles, simply drag a tile to an empty area of the Start Screen and a vertical grey line will appear indicating that when you release your finger a new group will be created.

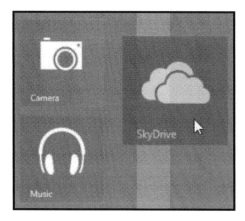

Key/Mouse – To relocate a tile, click and drag it to a new location. To create a new group of tiles, simply drag a tile to an empty area of the Start Screen and a vertical grey line will appear indicating that when you release the mouse a new group will be created.

Tip # 26 – Name & Arrange Groups

After a while as you add more apps and pinned items to the Start Screen it may begin to look a bit messy.

You can bring some order to this chaos by labelling your tile groups with names. Bring up the Start Screen App bar and then select **Customize**, a "Name Group" field will appear above each of your tile groups. Tap or click on each field and type in a description, then tap or click the **Customize** button again to finish.

Using Semantic Zoom you can also quickly rearrange the locations of your groups. Start by zooming out to see all your tile groups. Then drag up or down on a group to select it and move it to a new location.

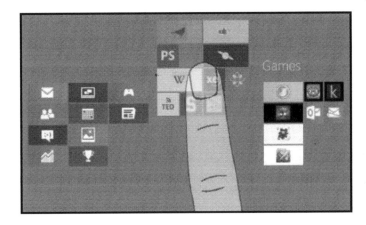

Tip # 27 – Managing Notifications

Windows 8 has a new Notification system that alerts you when important events take place, from operating system messages to updated information from apps that support notifications. These notifications can be either full screen messages or pop-up "toast" notifications that appear in the upper right corner of the screen. Tapping or clicking on the notification will launch the associated app. You can control how these notifications appear in a few different ways.

To adjust general notification settings, bring up the **Charms** menu and select **Settings**. Tap or click on **Change PC Settings**, select **Search and apps** and **Notifications**. Here you can change which apps use notifications, and turn off notification sounds, lock screen notifications, or all notifications!

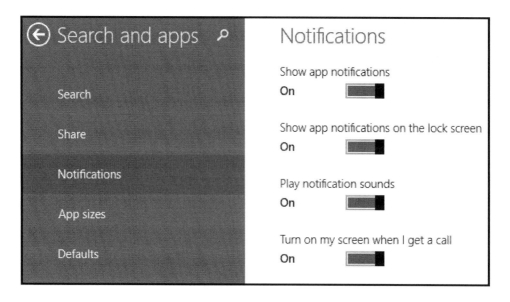

Another way you can adjust notifications is from directly within the apps themselves. For example, if you open the **Mail** app, then go to the **Charms** menu, select **Settings** and **Permissions**, you will see another notification switch.

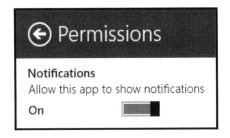

Also in some apps you can switch notifications on/off per account. So if you have multiple email accounts for example, you could set up Mail to receive notifications from only your most important account(s). Bring up the **Charms** menu, select **Settings** and **Accounts**. Then tap or click on an account and scroll down to see the notification dropdown list.

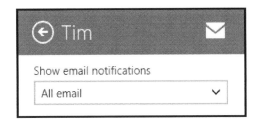

Finally, you can temporarily hide the notifications for a few hours while you're doing something like working or watching a movie and don't want to be interrupted. From the **Start Screen**, bring up the **Charms** menu and select **Settings**. Tap or click on **Notifications**, then you can choose to hide them for 1, 3 or 8 hours.

Tip # 28 – Adding Devices & Printers

Personalizing your computer wouldn't be complete without adding your devices and printers.

Touch – Bring up the **Charms** menu and tap **Search**. Select **Settings** and start typing "Devices and Printers", then tap to select it. You can choose to add a printer or other device and then follow the on-screen instructions.

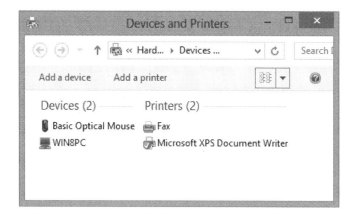

Key/Mouse – Press ⊞ + **W** and start typing "Devices and Printers", then click to select it. You can choose to add a printer or other device and then follow the on-screen instructions.

Chapter 3 – Modern Communications

In addition to Skype, Microsoft has designed a new suite of communication apps in the Modern UI, including the Mail, Calendar and People apps. The People app ties them all together and can be setup to integrate your email and social media contacts from various sources including Facebook, LinkedIn, Hotmail, Twitter and more.

The Mail app is a simple, streamlined email application that can be setup for use with most popular email services. The Calendar app gives you a nicely designed, crisp and clean layout for all your appointments.

In this chapter you'll learn how to setup and integrate your accounts and use some of the more interesting features of the new Windows 8 communication suite.

Tip # 29 – Adding An Account

Each of these communication apps (Mail, Calendar and People) lets you add accounts from popular email and social media services.

Touch – Open one of the apps, then bring up the **Charms** menu, tap **Settings** and **Accounts**. Tap **Add an account**, select the service you wish to add and follow the on-screen instructions.

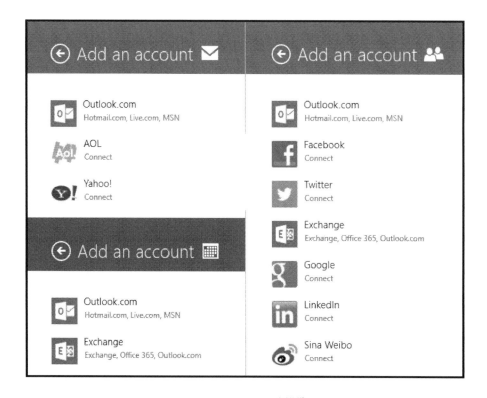

Key/Mouse – Open one of the app, then press ⊞ + **I** to bring up **Settings** and click on **Accounts**. Click **Add an account**, select the service you wish to add and follow the on-screen instructions.

Tip # 30 – Sorting Your Contacts

Depending on your personal preference, you might like to sort your contacts alphabetically by first name or by last name.

Touch – Open the People app, then bring up the **Charms** menu, tap **Settings** and **Options**. Then tap the **Sort my contacts by last name** switch to **Yes** or **No**.

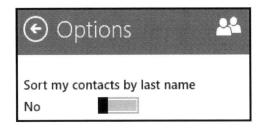

Key/Mouse – Open the People app, then press  + **I** to bring up **Settings** and click on **Options**. Then click the **Sort my contacts by last name** switch to **Yes** or **No**.

Tip # 31 – Mail Signature

If you write a lot of emails you might want to add an email signature to your account. This personal "sign off" line is added to the bottom of outgoing messages saving you a little bit of typing each time.

Touch – Open the Mail app, then bring up the **Charms** menu, tap **Settings** and **Accounts**. Select the account. Then tap the **Use an email signature** switch to **Yes** and type in your signature.

Use an email signature
Yes
Regards, Tim Sievers

Key/Mouse – Open the Mail app, then press + **I** to bring up **Settings** and click on **Accounts**. Then select the account. Click the **Use an email signature** switch to **Yes** and type in your signature.

Tip # 32 – Pin Individual Mail Folders

As well as pinning apps and file locations to the Start Screen you can also pin email folders. This is great if you have multiple email accounts because you can pin the individual folders from different accounts and jump straight to the account you want.

Touch – Open the Mail app, select the email folder, then swipe up a small way from the bottom of the screen to show the App bar. Tap **Manage folders** and select **Pin to Start**, type a name for the shortcut and/or tap the **Pin to Start** button to finish.

Key/Mouse – Open the Mail app, select the email folder, then right-click to bring up the App bar. Click on **Manage folders** and select **Pin to Start**, type a name for the shortcut and/or click the **Pin to Start** button to finish.

Tip # 33 – Email Formatting

The Mail app allows you to quickly add text formatting to your email messages. You can choose different font styles, sizes and colors, as well as highlight, bold, italic and underline options.

Tap or click within the body of the message, then swipe up a small way from the bottom of the screen or right-click to show the App bar. Then choose your favorite text options.

Tip # 34 – Getting Emotional About Icons

The Mail app in Windows 8 includes hundreds of picture icons called Emoticons. These tiny pictures are designed as a fun way to express how you're feeling and liven up your email messages.

Swipe or right-click to bring up the App bar. Select the **Emoticons** button, then tap or click the icons in the top row to choose different categories and tap or click to make a selection.

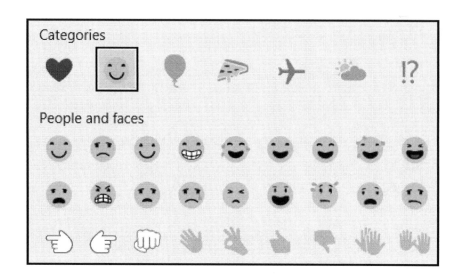

Tip # 35 – Colorful Calendars

The Calendar app will display events like birthdays, holidays and appointments in different colors. If you don't like the default options, you have a choice of 12 different colors.

Touch – Open the Calendar app, then bring up the **Charms** menu, tap **Settings** and **Options**. Then you can use the dropdown lists to choose different colors for your calendar events.

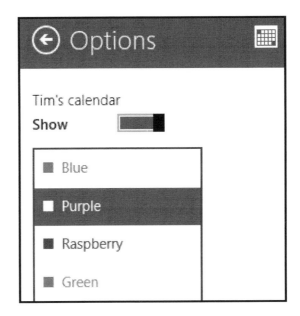

Key/Mouse – Open the Calendar app, then press + **I** to bring up **Settings** and select **Options**. Then you can use the dropdown lists to choose different colors for your calendar events.

Chapter 4 – Modern Day Apps

As well as the communication apps covered in the last chapter, Windows 8 comes with a variety of built-in apps designed for the Modern UI, including Maps, Reading List, Food & Drink, Health & Fitness, Photos, Weather, Finance, News, Sports, Travel, SkyDrive, Reader and Xbox Music, Video & Games. Many of these apps are integrated with the Bing search engine and bring together the latest data from all over the web. Sometimes called "Windows 8 apps" or "Modern UI apps", these new applications are designed to be touch-friendly and easy to use.

In this chapter we'll take a look at some of the best new features of these built-in Windows 8 apps.

Tip # 36 – Bird's Eye View

The Maps app in Windows 8 includes a new "Bird's Eye View" when you zoom in on a popular location. First find your location and change your **Map Style** to **Aerial View** via the App bar, then zoom in until the image switches to the 3D style Bird's Eye View. A new **Rotate**  button will appear on the right of the screen. You can use it to switch between four different angled views and an overhead view.

Tip # 37 – Finding Direction

Of course, maps are all about helping you find your way and the Maps app makes it easy to find directions from your current location, places that you "pinpoint" on the map or between any two addresses.

In the Maps app, to find your current location, just swipe or right-click to bring up the App bar, then tap or click on **My location**. To get directions to or from your current location, bring up the App bar and select the **Directions** button. If required, you can use the swap ↑↓ button to switch the "To" and "From" locations around, then type in the other location and tap or click the search → button.

To Pinpoint a location on the map, bring up the App bar and **tap & hold** or **click & hold** on the **Add a pin** button, then drag it to a location on the map and release. You can tap or click on the pin to select the **Directions** button, then type in the other location and tap or click the search ![button] button.

To simply find directions between to addresses, swipe or right-click to bring up the App bar, then tap or click on **Directions**. Type in the "From" and "To" addresses and tap or click the search ![button] button.

Tip # 38 – Reading List

The new Reading List app in Windows 8.1 allows you to bookmark articles you want to read later when you have more time. You can bookmark articles from websites and many other apps as well. To bookmark an article just bring up the **Charms** menu, tap **Share** and if available, select **Reading List**. Then select the **Add** button.

Once you have bookmarked a few articles you can simply access your Reading List from the Start Screen or the Apps View.

Tip # 39 – Food & Drink

For anyone who likes to cook, the Food & Drink app is brilliant! It allows you view recipes, create shopping lists, plans your meals, view cooking tips and get advice from celebrity chefs. It also includes guides for wine and cocktail drinks. But perhaps the best feature is the **Hands-Free Mode**.

If your Windows 8 computer has a webcam you can use simple hand gestures while cooking to flip through step-by-step recipe guides without getting sticky fingers all over your machine.

To try it out, open a recipe and select the **Hands-Free Mode** option at the bottom of the screen. Tap or click the **Allow** button to let the app use your webcam, then slowly move your hand from right to left in front of your webcam to flip forward through the recipe guide. Reverse the gesture from left to right to go backwards.

Tip # 40 – Health & Fitness

If you spend too much time in the Food & Drink app, then you might need the Health & Fitness app to keep you in shape! This app provides nutritional information, fitness videos, exercise examples, medical news and a "symptom checker" to help you diagnose health issues. You can also keep track of your diet, health and exercise information.

The Diet Tracker, for example, is a great way to measure your daily intake of Calories. Simply tap or click on the **FOOD** button next to a meal and start typing the name of the food you had for that meal, select it from the results list and select the portion size from the dropdown list, then tap or click the **DONE** button. Repeat this for every meal and you'll get the total calories for that day.

Tip # 41 – Set & Shuffle

The Photos app allows you to set a photo to the Lock screen or the apps Start Screen tile. You can also choose to show a random shuffle of your images on the Start Screen tile.

Touch – Open the Photos app, select an image, then swipe to bring up the App bar. Tap to set the image to the Lock screen or Photos tile. To turn the photo shuffle On or Off, bring up the **Charms** menu, tap **Settings** and **Options**. Then tap the **Shuffle photos on the Photos tile** switch.

Key/Mouse – Open the Photos app, select an image, then right-click to bring up the App bar. Click to set the image to the Lock screen or Photos tile. To turn the photo shuffle On or Off, press ▦ + I to bring up **Settings** and select **Options**. Then click on the **Shuffle photos on the Photos tile** switch.

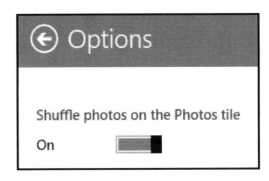

Tip # 42 – Crop & Rotate

The Photos app also lets you do some basic picture editing. You can simply rotate an image by selecting it, bringing up the App bar and tapping or clicking on the **Rotate** button to turn the image clockwise, 90 degrees at a time.

To crop an image, tap or click the **Crop** button in the App bar and drag on the selection handles to highlight the area you want to keep, then tap or click the **Apply** button.

Tip # 43 – Weather Watch

The Weather app lets you search and save your favorite places, so you can quickly access them via the Places button, which appears at the top of the screen when you bring up the App bars.

Open the Weather app, then tap or click the **Search** icon in the top right-hand corner. Type in a location and select a result. Bring up the App bars, then tap or click the **Add**  button to save the location. Now when you select **Places** from the top App bar, you will see a list of your favorite locations.

Tip # 44 – A Greater Forecast

The Weather app in Windows 8 is very comprehensive; you can pan or scroll to see daily and hourly forecasts, detailed weather maps and historical averages for temperatures, rainfall, sunshine and snow. However you can display even more data by tapping or clicking the Show More ⬇ button, below the daily forecasts, to see details of Wind Speed, Visibility, Humidity and Barometric pressure.

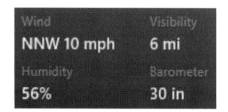

Tip # 45 – Watchlist

The Finance app is another surprisingly detailed application that will be a must for market watchers. You can check charts and statistics for stocks and the major indices from around the world by day, week, month and year, get loan and currency rate data and check the latest economic news all in one place. The best way to get started is by setting up a custom Watchlist.

To add a stock to your watchlist, open the Finance app, pan or scroll to the Watchlist, then tap or click the Add ⊕ button and type in a company name or stock symbol, tap or click **Add** or select a suggested stock from the dropdown list. To remove an item from the Watchlist, just **long-press** or **right-click** on the stock and select the **Delete** ⊗ button.

WATCHLIST ▸

MSFT	Microsoft Corporation
▲ 29.20	+0.25 **+0.86%**

AMZN	Amazon.com
▼ 242.36	-1.86 **-0.76%**

GOOG	Google Inc
▼ 744.75	-6.73 **-0.90%**

⊕

Tip # 46 – Custom News

The News app sources information from hundreds of the worlds leading news sites. You can customize your news topics to get the news you want.

Open the News app, then swipe or right-click to bring up the App bar. Tap or click on **Topics**, select **Add A Topic** and start typing a news topic, tap or click **Add** or select a suggested topic from the dropdown list. To remove a news topic, first swipe or right-click to bring up the App bar and select the **Remove** button. Then long-press or right-click on the topic and tap or click the **Remove** button.

Tip # 47 – Playing Favorites

The Sports app covers many popular sports and allows you to add your favorite teams to personalize your Sporting news.

To add one of your favorite teams, open the Sports app, pan or scroll to **Favorite Teams**, then tap or click the Add ⊕ button and type in a team name, tap or click **Add** or select a suggested team from the dropdown list. To remove a team, just long-press or **right-click** on the team and select the **Delete** ✕ button.

Tip # 48 – Panoramic Views

The Travel app includes a great feature that allows you to view 360 degree Panoramas of popular tourist locations and give you some sense of what the place would be like to visit.

Open the Travel app from the Apps View, then tap or click in the **Search** field in the top right-hand corner and type in a travel destination, like Paris for example. Then tap or click the **Search** icon and select a result. Pan or scroll until you see the **Panoramas** heading. Select a location, tap & hold or click & hold, then drag on the screen, left & right or up & down, to see the full panorama.

Tip # 49 – Flight Status

The Travel app also includes a real gem of a feature called Flight Status, which lets you check if a flight is running on time.

Just open the Travel app and bring up the App Bar, then select **Flights** and tap or click on the **Status** option. Enter the flight details and select **Get Status**.

Tip # 50 – Taking to the Sky

When you login with a Microsoft account, you'll have access to Microsoft's cloud storage solution called SkyDrive, which lets you upload, sync and share files across all your devices. SkyDrive is integrated into Windows 8.1 and gives you a choice of places to save your files, either **This PC** or **SkyDrive**.

You can also get SkyDrive apps for Windows Phone, Android, Mac, iPhone and iPad. Plus the website version of SkyDrive gives you the ability to create Office documents in the Cloud.

To access SkyDrive directly from the Internet, go to http://skydrive.com. To create an Office document within SkyDrive just select the Create dropdown list and choose a file type.

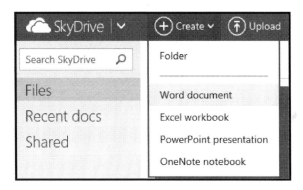

Tip # 51 – PDF Notes & Highlights

The Reader app lets you view both PDF & XPS files. You can easily view two pages at a time, rotate the pages, search for words or phrases and even use Semantic Zoom, but the best feature is the ability to highlight text and make notes.

Tap & drag or **click & drag** to select a section of text, then tap or right-click on the selection to choose **Highlight** or **Add a note**. When you close the file, choose **Yes** to save your changes.

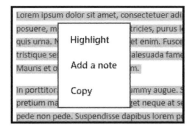

Note: Some PDF files have security settings that don't permit notes & highlights, to check if you can add notes & highlights to a PDF file, bring up the App bar, select **More** and then select **Info**. Under **Permissions**, you should see a tick next to **Add notes and highlight**.

Tip # 52 – Xbox Profile

To unlock the full benefits of the Xbox Music, Video and Games apps, like for example, free music streaming from a catalog of tens of millions of songs, then you'll need to sign up for a free Xbox Profile.

Open any one of these apps and bring up the **Settings** charm. Select **Account** and tap or click the sign in button.

Chapter 5 – Desktop Productivity

Microsoft has made a number of visual changes to the Desktop in Windows 8. Gone is the graphically intense "Aero" styling with its translucent glass window borders, reflections and other visual effects. Edges have been squared off, shadows and gradients have been removed, and controls have been flattened to create a cleaner, simpler look & feel.

Most of the changes to the Desktop may seem minor compared to the dramatic addition of the Modern UI covered in the previous 4 chapters, but there are a few noteworthy improvements.

In this chapter we'll take a look at these improvements and some of my favorite features of the Desktop.

Tip # 53 – Chameleon Taskbar & Borders

While most of the theme settings in the Desktop remain unchanged, you'll notice that when you change the Desktop Background your Taskbar & Window Borders will also change automatically to blend in with the Background Image. This new trick can be fun at first, but you could soon get sick of it if you have chosen a rotating Background theme. Follow these steps to change this setting:

Long-press or right-click an empty area of the Desktop and select **Personalize**. Then tap or click on **Color** and make a selection.

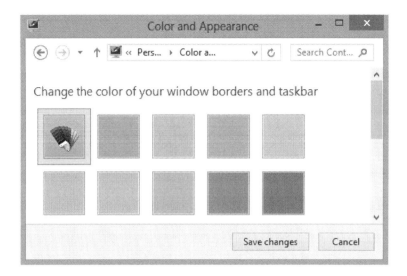

Note: You can also change the color intensity and select **Show color mixer** to adjust hue, saturation and brightness.

Tip # 54 – Change the Text Size of Individual Items

Windows Vista introduced a feature that allowed users to scale the items on the screen to make them easier to read on high-resolution displays. This was a great addition because you could easily increase the size of text and images on the screen without compromising the screen resolution. The only problem was that you couldn't choose which text items to increase, it was "all or nothing" and in some cases different items didn't fit correctly on the screen or overlapped other items. Windows 8 gives you a finer level of control by allowing you to adjust the size of individual text items.

Long-press or right-click an empty area of the Desktop and select **Screen resolution**. Then tap or click on **Make text and other items larger or smaller**. Under the **Change only the text size** section, use the dropdown boxes to select specific items and then adjust the font settings as required.

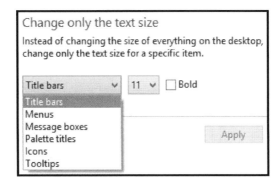

Tip # 55 – SkyDrive Settings

SkyDrive can synchronize your local computer settings across all your Windows 8 PCs. It will also save and upload your files & photos by default. To adjust these settings and more:

Touch – Bring up the **Charms** menu and tap **Settings**, then select **Change PC Settings** and **SkyDrive**.

Key/Mouse – Press ⊞ + **I**, then select **Change PC Settings** and **SkyDrive**.

Here you can adjust your default save location, choose whether you want to upload photos & videos, select various PC Sync settings and adjust your upload/download settings over metered internet connections.

Tip # 56 – Snap Comparison

With Desktop Snap you can easily arrange two windows side by side for moving files around, comparing documents or just multitasking.

Touch – Simply tap & drag the title bar of a window beyond the left-hand or right-hand sides of the screen until your finger hits the edge of the screen, release and the window will expand to fit half the screen. Drag another window to the other side and the two windows will be perfectly tiled side by side. To restore a window to its original size just drag the title bar away from the top of the screen and release.

Key/Mouse – Use the keyboard shortcuts, ⊞ + **Left Arrow** or ⊞ + **Right Arrow**, to snap an active window to either side of the screen.

Note: Because the Modern UI treats the Desktop as a single app, you can combine Desktop Snapping with Modern Snapping (see Tip # 11) to get more apps on the screen at once!

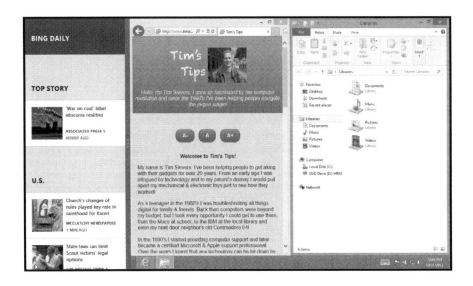

Tip # 57 – Make It Snappy

Desktop Snap also makes it easy to stretch, maximize and restore a window to its original size.

Touch – To make a window taller so you can see more detail on the screen simply drag the bottom edge of the window until your finger hits the edge of the Taskbar, release and the window will stretch to the top and bottom of the screen. To maximize the active window, drag the title bar of the window to the top of the screen until your finger hits the edge of the screen, release and the window will expand to full screen. To restore a window to its original size just drag the title bar away from the top of the screen and release.

Key/Mouse – Use the following shortcuts; ⊞ + **Shift** + **Up Arrow** to stretch a window. ⊞ + **Up Arrow** to maximize the window. ⊞ + **Down Arrow** to minimize the window. ⊞ + **M** to minimize all windows. ⊞ + **Shift** + **M** to restore all windows. ⊞ + **Home** to minimize all windows except for the active one and repeat to restore all windows.

Tip # 58 – Shake It Up

Desktop Shake allows you to quickly minimize all other windows on your Desktop except the one you're shaking. Simply grab (tap & hold or click & hold) the title bar of a window and shake it from side to side. All other open windows will minimize to the Taskbar. To restore the other windows just grab and shake the window title bar again.

Tip # 59 – Have A Peek

Desktop Peek allows you to quickly see your Desktop without closing or minimizing all your open windows.

Touch – Tap & hold your finger in the very bottom right-hand corner of the Desktop next to the clock. If a menu appears, tap the **Peek at desktop** option, then tap & hold again to see a preview of the Desktop. Any open windows should fade away and reveal the Desktop, just release your finger to restore the open windows.

Key/Mouse – From the Desktop, use the keyboard shortcut, ⊞ + , (comma) to preview the Desktop, just release the Windows logo key to restore the previous view or use the keyboard shortcut, ⊞ + **D** to Show the Desktop (Minimize all your open Desktop windows) and repeat the shortcut to restore all windows.

You can also use these shortcuts from the Modern UI. The first time you press the ⊞ + **D** shortcut it will switch you to the Desktop, then repeat to Show the Desktop and once more to restore all windows. Pressing the Windows logo key by itself will return you to the Start Screen.

Tip # 60 – Projecting Your Vision

Connecting your machine on a Projector or an extra monitor is simple in Windows 8.

Touch – Long-press on an empty area of the Desktop and tap **Screen resolution**. Then tap on **Project to a second screen**. Then choose your preferred setup.

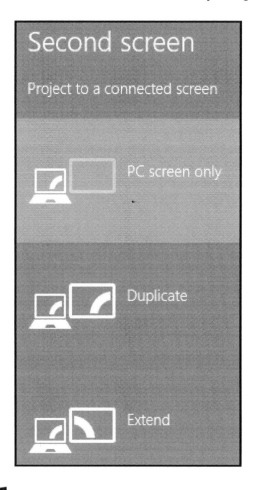

Key/Mouse – Press ⊞ + **P**. Then choose your preferred setup.

Tip # 61 – Multi-Monitor Taskbar

Windows 8 includes some improvements to the way the Taskbar works when you have multiple displays connected to your device.

Touch – Long-press on an empty area of the Taskbar to bring up the options menu, then tap **Properties**. Under the **Multiple displays** section you can change the appearance of the Taskbar.

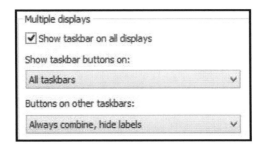

Key/Mouse – Right-click on an empty area of the Taskbar to bring up the options menu, then click **Properties**. Under the **Multiple displays** section you can change the appearance of the Taskbar.

Note: When using multiple monitors, you can press ⊞ + **Shift** + **Left Arrow** and ⊞ + **Shift** + **Right Arrow** to move the active Desktop window between monitors.

Chapter 6 –   Exploring the Ribbon

In Windows 8 the file management app formerly known as "Windows Explorer" gets a new name, "File Explorer". But the big change is the addition of a Microsoft Office style Ribbon, replacing the old Menu System.

The Ribbon is hidden or minimized by default. To show or expand the Ribbon, tap or click on the down arrow ☑ next to the Help ❓ button in the upper right-hand corner of the File Explorer window.

The Ribbon was designed to enhanced productivity by grouping related commands together in tabs. For many people familiar with previous versions of Explorer, the Ribbon can be a bit scary at first, but most of the old Menu commands can still be found by exploring the Ribbon.

In this chapter we'll take a closer look at some of the main features of the Ribbon and a couple of other additions to File Explorer, so you can get up to speed quickly.

Tip # 62 – The File Tab

The File tab replaces the old File menu. It allows you to open a new File Explorer window and shows a list of your most frequently accessed file locations. Plus you can get quick access to the command prompt and Windows PowerShell.

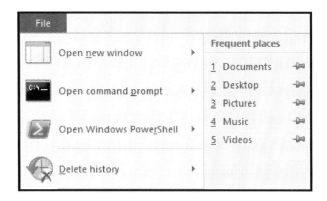

Tip # 63 – The Home Tab

In File Explorer, over 80 % of the most commonly used File Management commands are found in the Home tab. Just tap or click on **Home** to see the Home tab. Here you can copy, paste, create, open, move, delete, rename and manage your files and folders. The Home tab also includes some handy shortcuts like "Move to", "Copy to" and "Copy path" which will save a file path to the clipboard. Plus a new command called History, which is covered later in Tip # 86.

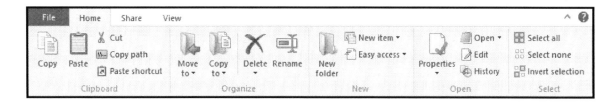

Tip # 64 – The Share Tab

The Share tab allows you to burn, print, fax, compress and email your files. As well as, applying network-sharing and advanced security permissions.

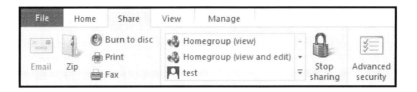

Tip # 65 – The View Tab

The View tab allows you to customize File Explorer and get it looking the way you like it. You can change what's displayed in the Navigation pane or turn it off, show the Preview pane or Details pane, change icon sizes, group and sort items, add columns, show file name extensions, show hidden files and hide selected items. Plus the **Options** button gives you access to Folder & Search options.

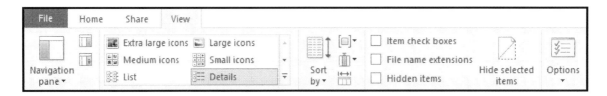

Tip # 66 – The Homegroup, Computer & Network Tabs

The Ribbon also hides a bunch of contextual tabs that appear in the context of specific files, folders, locations and tasks. For example, selecting **Homegroup** in the Navigation pane will replace the Home tab with a Homegroup tab, which allows you to share libraries and devices with your homegroup.

Selecting your computer in the Navigation pane will replace the Home tab with a **Computer** tab, which allows you to perform tasks like accessing media, mapping a network drive and managing your computer.

Selecting **Network** in the Navigation pane will replace the Home tab with a Network tab, which allows you to open network connections and configure network devices and settings.

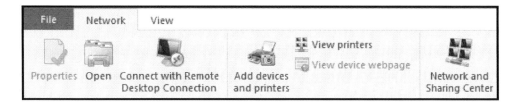

Tip # 67 – The Search, Library & Drive Tools

Selecting the Search field in File Explorer will bring up the Search Tools contextual tab. Here you can quickly adjust and filter your search settings, then save your Search details for future use.

Selecting a library will activate the Library Tools contextual tab, which lets you manage and optimize your Libraries.

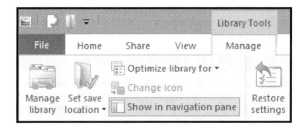

Selecting a drive will activate the Drive Tools contextual tab, which provides tools for working with removable storage devices and hard drives.

Tip # 68 – The Picture, Music & Video Tools

The Picture Tools contextual tab lets you rotate your images, play a slideshow and set the desktop background. The Music & Video tabs have basic playback & playlist options.

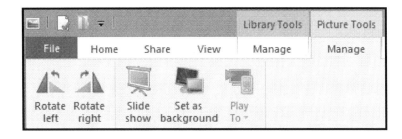

Tip # 69 – The Only Way Is UP!

A feature not seen since Windows XP, the much-loved **Up** button finally returns in Windows 8. The Up button takes you up one level in the directory structure. You can tap or click on the Up button which is located next to the Back and Forward buttons directly under the Ribbon. Or use the keyboard shortcut: **Alt + Up Arrow**

Tip # 70 – Quick Access Toolbar

Sitting just above the Ribbon is another new feature that has made its way from Microsoft Office to File Explorer, the Quick Access Toolbar. You can add undo, redo, delete and rename shortcuts to the Quick Access Toolbar and change its location from above the Ribbon to below by tapping or clicking on the Customize

 button and making your preferred selections.

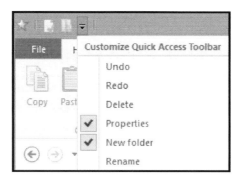

You can also add your favorite commands from the Ribbon. Just **long-press** or **right-click** on a command, then select **Add to Quick Access Toolbar**.

Chapter 7 – The Two Interfaces of Internet Explorer

In Windows 8, Internet Explorer comes with two different interfaces, the traditional Desktop interface and a new Modern UI interface. At first this can seem a bit strange and you could be forgiven for thinking they were two totally different browsers, but the best way to understand the difference is to think of the Desktop interface as the fully-featured advanced mode and the Modern interface as the touch-friendly streamlined mode.

In this chapter you'll learn how to get the most out of your Windows 8 browsing experience.

Tip # 71 – Put It On A Tab

Tab Browsing allows you to quickly switch between multiple websites. This works the same way in the Desktop mode as before but it's a little different in the Modern interface. To check it out, start Internet Explorer from the Start Screen.

Touch – To create a new Tab, swipe inwards from the bottom or top edge of the screen to show the App bar, then tap on the **New Tab** button. To switch between Tabs, swipe inwards from the bottom or top edge of the screen to show the App bar, then tap on another Tab.

Key/Mouse – To create a new Tab, right-click to bring up the App bar and click on the **New Tab** button or use the shortcut **Ctrl + T**. To switch between Tabs, right-click to bring up the App bar, then click on another Tab.

Tip # 72 – Modern Favorites

With it's simple and clean full screen appearance the Modern interface of Internet Explorer can leave you wondering "did someone forget to add the buttons?" and "how do I access my Favorites?" Actually most of the commands, like the Favorites button, are hidden away in the App bar. To access your Favorites:

Touch – Swipe inwards from the bottom or top edge of the screen to show the App bar, then tap on the **Favorites** button. Use the **Add to favorites** button to save new favorites and the **Tabs** button to switch back to your Tabs.

Key/Mouse – Right-click to bring up the App bar and click on the **Favorites**

button. Use the **Add to favorites** button to save new favorites and the **Tabs** button to switch back to your Tabs.

Tip # 73 – Your Favorite Pin-Ups

Internet Explorer allows you to "Pin" websites to the Start Screen for easy access.

To Pin a website, start Internet Explorer in the Modern interface. Swipe or right-click to show the App bar, select the Favorites button and tap or click on the

Pin site button, then select **Pin to Start**.

Tip # 74 – Moving Back & Forward by going Side to Side

The Modern interface of Internet Explorer includes the normal Back & Forward buttons in the App bar that allow you to move back to a previous page or forward to a page you just left. But you don't have to bring up the App bar to do this.

Touch – Simply swipe from left to right across the screen to go back, or from right to left to go forward. (Just don't start from the edge of the screen or you'll accidentally bring up the Charms menu or switch to a different app!)

Key/Mouse – Move the mouse pointer to the left of the screen to see a Back button, or move to the right to see a Forward button.

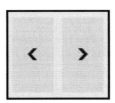

Tip # 75 – For Your Eyes Only

InPrivate Browsing lets you browse the web without leaving behind a history of where you've been. You can start InPrivate Browsing from either the Modern or Desktop interfaces.

Touch – To enable InPrivate Browsing from the Desktop, start Internet Explorer, then tap on the **Tools** ⚙ icon and go to **Safety > InPrivate Browsing**.

To enable InPrivate Browsing from the Start Screen, tap on the Internet Explorer tile and swipe to show the App bar, then tap on the **Tab tools** ⬤ button and select **New InPrivate Tab**.

Key/Mouse – To enable InPrivate Browsing from the Desktop, right-click on the Internet Explorer icon in the Taskbar and select **Start InPrivate Browsing** from the Jump List.

To enable InPrivate Browsing from the Start Screen, click on the Internet Explorer tile and right-click to show the App bar, then click on the **Tab tools** button and select **New InPrivate Tab**.

Note: Each InPrivate Browsing session only lasts until you close the browser window.

Tip # 76 – Switch to Advanced mode

If you started using the Modern interface of Internet Explorer and then decide you should be using the Desktop interface, you can easily switch without losing the webpage you have open.

Swipe or right-click to show the App bar and tap or click on the **Page tools** button, then select **View in the desktop**.

Tip # 77 – Block the Pop-Up Blocker

Pop-up windows are painful & annoying. Internet Explorer and most modern browsers now block all pop-ups by default, saving you from dealing with them, but some web designers still insist on using pop-ups. If you really need to see a pop-up window on a website you can turn the Blocker off.

From the Desktop, start Internet Explorer, then tap or click on the **Tools**  icon and tap or click **Internet options**. Select the **Privacy** tab and uncheck the **Turn on Pop-up Blocker** checkbox.

Pop-up Blocker
☑ Turn on Pop-up Blocker

Tip # 78 – Using Add-Ons

The new Modern interface of Internet Explorer is "add-on free", so you can't install third-party toolbars or other browser add-on software. This was done by design to keep the interface clean and simple. If the website you're viewing requires an add-on, you'll need to switch to the Desktop interface. To manage add-ons:

From the Desktop, start Internet Explorer, then tap or click on the **Tools** icon and tap or click **Manage add-ons**.

Tip # 79 – Safe Searching

Windows 8 includes a SafeSearch feature that filters out adult content. The default setting is **Moderate**, which filters images and videos but not text.

Touch – To adjust this feature, bring up the **Charms** menu, tap **Settings** and **Change PC settings**. Select **Search and apps**, then **Search** and scroll down to see the **SafeSearch** options. Then make a selection.

Key/Mouse – To adjust this feature, press ⊞ + **I** to bring up **Settings** and click on **Change PC settings**. Select **Search and apps**, then **Search** and scroll down to see the **SafeSearch** options. Then make a selection.

Tip # 80 – Take Out The Trash

Over time all the little files that make up each webpage that you visit, create a bit of a mess on your computer and start slowing things down. To delete these files:

From the Desktop, start Internet Explorer, then tap or click on the **Tools** icon and select **Internet options**. Under the **Browsing history** section tap or click the **Delete...** button then select **Delete** again.

Tip # 81 – Save It For Later

The Internet is almost always available these days, but not everywhere you go. If you're travelling and don't have time to read a whole web page, you can save the webpage locally to your computer when you're online, and read it later when you're offline.

From the Desktop, start Internet Explorer, then tap or click on the **Tools** icon and go to **File > Save as...** choose a location to save the webpage and give it a name, then tap or click **Save**.

Note: Only the individual page that you are viewing will be saved, not the whole website. If the article or information you want to read offline is on multiple pages you will need to save each page individually.

Chapter 8 – Safety & Security

The growth of the Internet has put the world at your finger tips; you can bank and shop online, play games, use social networks and access information and entertainment like never before.

Unfortunately the growth in cyber crime has been equally amazing. Statistics from the U.S. Justice Dept show that in the year 2000 they received 16,000+ official complaints of cyber crime, compared to 300,000+ in 2011 with an estimated value of $485 million.

Microsoft has been very focussed on security since Windows XP Service Pack 2 and built many improvements into Windows Vista and Windows 7.

Windows 8 builds on these security enhancements. You can protect against viruses and spyware, setup easy to use passwords, keep your software up to date, solve issues and backup your important data. You can also use Parental Controls to set limits on your children's computer usage.

This chapter introduces you to these and other techniques to help you safe guard your computer.

Tip # 82 – Taking Action

In Windows 8, the Action Center allows you to manage your Anti-virus, User Account Control, Windows Update and Internet Security settings. The Action Center also helps you perform maintenance, troubleshoot and fix computer problems.

The Action Center alerts you when something requires your attention. Important items, labeled in red, could cause major problems if not addressed. Items labeled in yellow are less important but highly recommended suggestions.

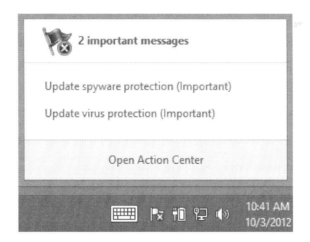

You can see if there are any messages in the Action Center by checking the icon in the Notification Area on the Desktop. To access the Action Center:

Touch – Bring up the **Charms** menu and tap **Search**. Select **Settings** and start typing "Action Center", then tap to select it.

Key/Mouse – Click on the Flag icon  in the Notification Area of the Desktop, then click **Open Action Center**.

Tip # 83 – Defending Windows

Protecting your computer against malicious software (malware) like viruses and spyware is an ongoing battle. Malware infections can delete data, steal personal information and take complete control of your computer. In Windows 8, Microsoft has included built-in Anti-Malware protection called Windows Defender. Previously just an Anti-spyware program, Windows Defender has been beefed up to include Anti-virus protection. Of course, you can still choose to install your preferred security software, but unlike previous versions, Windows 8 gives you a basic level of security from the very beginning. To run a scan with Windows Defender:

Touch – Bring up the **Charms** menu, tap **Search** and start typing "Windows Defender", then tap to select it. Choose from Quick, Full and Custom scan types then tap the **Scan now** button.

Key/Mouse – Press 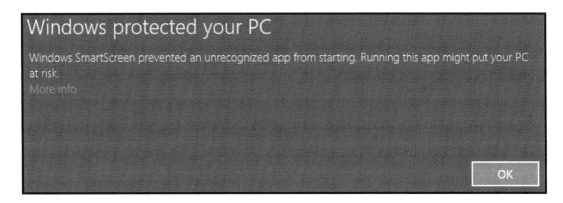 + **Q** and start typing "Windows Defender", then click on it. Choose from Quick, Full and Custom scan types then click the **Scan now** button.

Note: Malware infections generally come from email attachments, malicious websites, downloading "free" software such as screen savers and search toolbars or from music and file sharing networks.

Tip # 84 – Smart Screening

Windows 8 includes a filtering technology, called SmartScreen, which protects you from malicious apps and websites. SmartScreen was previously available as part of Internet Explorer 9 but now works system wide in Windows 8.

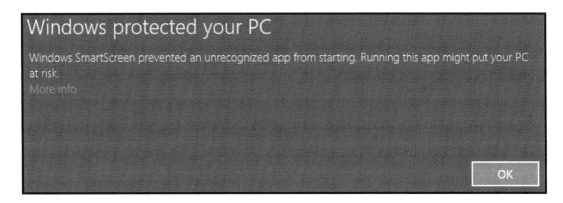

Windows protected your PC

Windows SmartScreen prevented an unrecognized app from starting. Running this app might put your PC at risk.

More info

OK

SmartScreen is usually configured during Windows installation, but you can adjust the filter settings at any time.

Touch – Bring up the **Charms** menu and tap **Search**. Select **Settings** and start typing "Action Center", then tap to select it. Tap on **Change Windows SmartScreen settings**.

Key/Mouse – Click on the Flag icon  in the Notification Area of the Desktop, then click **Open Action Center**. Click on **Change Windows SmartScreen settings**.

Tip # 85 – Keeping It Updated

Keeping your computer up to date with the latest security patches is one of the best ways to stay protected. To update your computer:

Touch – Go to the Action Center. Then tap on **Windows Update** in the bottom left-hand corner. Tap on any **important updates** and select **Install**.

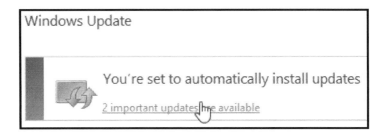

Key/Mouse – Go to the Action Center. Then click on **Windows Update** in the bottom left-hand corner. Click on any **important updates** and select **Install**.

Tip # 86 – File History

Windows 8 includes a new backup system called File History. When set up to an external drive or network location it will automatically backup your files on a regular basis and allow you to "go back in time" to restore a older version of a file. To configure File History:

Touch – Bring up the **Charms** menu and tap **Search**. Select **Settings** and start typing "File History", then tap to select it. Tap on **Select drive** and choose an external backup drive or add a network location, then tap **OK**. Tap **Turn on** and the first backup will begin. Under **Advanced settings** you can choose how often the backup occurs and how long to keep the files. To restore a file, you can either use the **History** button on the **Home Tab** in **File Explorer** or go to **Settings** in the **Search charm** and type "restore", then select **Restore your files with File History**.

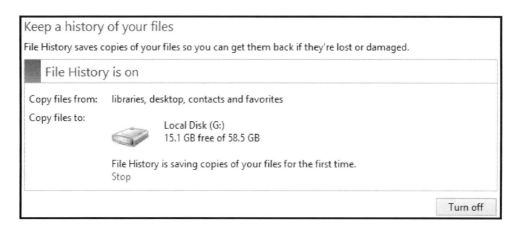

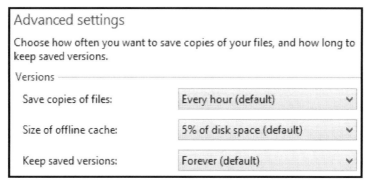

Key/Mouse – Press ⊞ + **W** and start typing "File History", then click to select it. Click **Select drive** and choose an external backup drive or add a network location, then click **OK**. Click the **Turn on** button and the first backup will begin. Under **Advanced settings** you can choose how often the backup occurs and how long to keep the files. To restore a file, you can either use the **History** button on the **Home Tab** in **File Explorer** or go to **Settings** in the **Search charm** and type "restore", then select **Restore your files with File History**.

Tip # 87 – Exercising Self Control

User Account Control (UAC) was first introduced in Windows Vista. UAC is a form of Authorization Security similar to that found in other operating systems like Linux or Unix. It was designed to stop viruses and spyware from taking complete control of the system. Even when logged on as an Administrator, UAC will ask you for permission whenever a change is made to the system. To adjust settings for UAC:

Touch – Go to the Action Center and tap on **Change User Account Control settings**. You can use the slider to select the setting you prefer and tap **OK**.

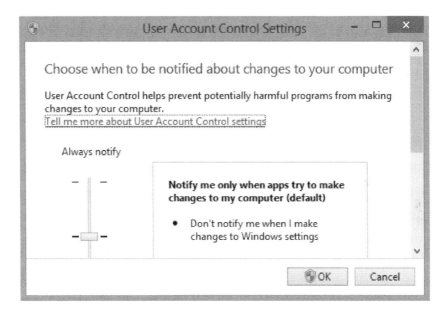

Key/Mouse – Go to the Action Center and click on **Change User Account Control settings**. You can use the slider to select the setting you prefer and click **OK**.

Note: UAC can be annoying and difficult for most Windows Users to get used to, but it is generally recommended that you keep the default setting and become more aware of what gets installed on your computer for your own protection.

Tip # 88 – Picture Passwords

Windows 8 allows you to draw a series of gestures on a picture as an alternative password.

Touch – Bring up the **Charms** menu and tap **Search**. Select **Settings** and start typing "Picture Password", then select **Set up picture password** and tap on the **Add** button under the **Picture password** option. Sign in with your normal password then choose a picture. Draw three gestures on your picture using any combination of circles, straight lines and taps. Then repeat to confirm.

Key/Mouse – Press ⊞ + **W** and start typing "Picture Password", then select **Set up picture password** and click on the **Add** button under the **Picture password** option. Sign in with your normal password then choose a picture. Using the mouse you can draw the following gestures:

- Straight lines – Click and drag the mouse pointer to draw a line, release to finish.
- Circles – Click and drag to draw a circle.
- Dot – Just click to create a single dot.

Use any combination of these gestures to draw a password on your picture. Then repeat to confirm.

Congratulations!

You've successfully created your picture password. Use it the next time you sign in to Windows.

Tip # 89 – Parental Controls

Windows 8 includes Parental Controls that let you set rules for your kids such as which games they can play, the hours during which they can use the computer and you can even stop them from using certain apps. To enable Parental Controls:

Bring up the **Search Charm** and start typing "Family Safety", then select it. To setup a new account for a child, tap or click on the **Accounts** option and select **Add an account**. Then select **Add a child's account**. Enter the account details and when you're finished, tap or click on **Manage Family Safety settings online**. Login and select the child's account. Here you can setup time limits, app & game restrictions, web filtering and also view activity reports.

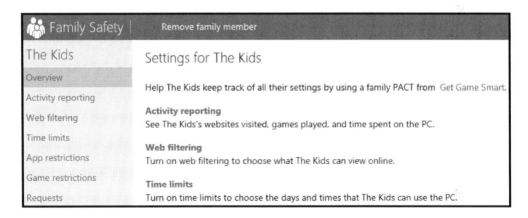

Note: If you have multiple Windows 8 devices you should setup a Microsoft Account for your children and then these settings will be synchronized across all your devices.

Chapter 9 – Advanced Bits & Bytes

Windows 8 makes it easy for you to recover your system if it crashes or becomes unstable, force apps to exit, change accessibility settings, change power settings, manage space & app updates and even reset your machine back to factory defaults.

In this chapter you'll learn how to use some of the advanced features in Windows 8.

Tip # 90 – Mounting ISO files

Windows 8 gives you the ability to mount ISO image files as a virtual CD/DVD disc, directly in File Explorer.

From the Desktop, start File Explorer, then navigate to the ISO file and simply double-tap or double-click on it to mount the ISO file as a virtual CD/DVD disc. When you're finished using the ISO file you can go to the Drive Tools contextual tab and "Eject" the virtual disc.

Note: You can also mount Virtual Hard Disk (VHD) files.

Tip # 91 – You have the Power

Depending on the hardware you have, Windows 8 offers a range of power management options. To change the power settings in Windows 8:

Touch – Bring up the **Charms** menu and tap **Search**. Select **Settings** and start typing "Power Options", then tap to select it. Here you can adjust various settings including brightness, display, sleep and power button options.

Key/Mouse – Press ⊞ + **W** and start typing "Power Options", then click on it. Here you can adjust various settings including brightness, display, sleep and power button options.

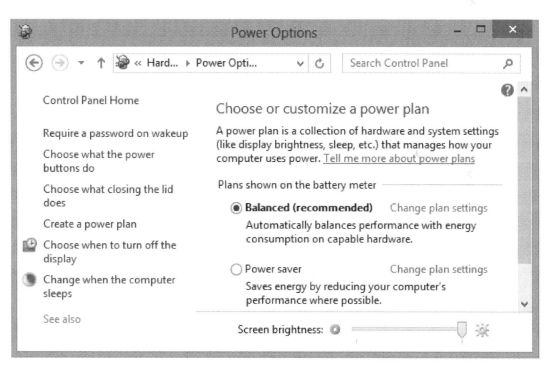

Tip # 92 – Task Master

If you have an app that stops working and locks up, Windows 8 will attempt to automatically correct the problem and save your changes, but if Windows can't fix the problem, you can manually force the app to close.

Touch – Bring up the **Charms** menu, tap **Search** and start typing "Task Manager", then tap to select it. In the "More Details" view select the **Processes** tab, select the app & tap **End Task**.

Key/Mouse – Press **Ctrl + Shift + Esc** to bring up the Task Manager, then on the **Processes** tab (In the "More Details" view) select the app & click **End Task**.

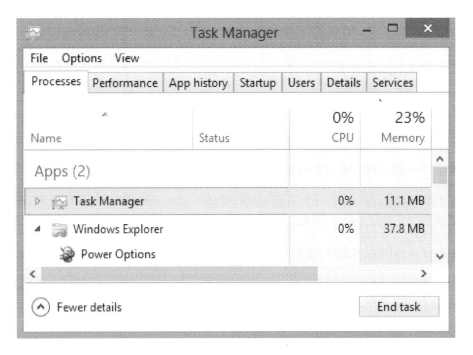

Tip # 93 – Take It Easy

In Windows 8, the full accessibility controls are found in the Ease of Access Center. You can adjust settings, make things easier to see, turn on the narrator and more. To open the Ease of Access Center:

Touch – Bring up the **Charms** menu and tap **Search**. Start typing "Ease of Access Center", then tap to select it.

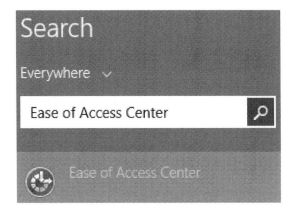

Key/Mouse – Use the keyboard shortcut, ⊞ + U

Tip # 94 – Custom Narrator

You can choose from 3 different narrator voices and adjust their speed, pitch and volume.

Touch – Bring up the **Charms** menu, tap **Search** and start typing "Narrator", then tap to select it. On the Desktop, tap the **Narrator Settings** window in the **Taskbar** and select **Voice**. You can use the dropdown box to select a different voice and use the sliders to make any required adjustments.

Key/Mouse – Press 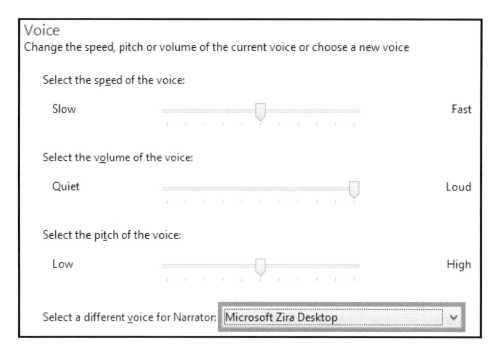 + **Enter** to start the Narrator. On the Desktop, select the **Narrator Settings** window in the **Taskbar** and click the **Voice** option. You can use the dropdown box to select a different voice and use the sliders to make any required adjustments.

Tip # 95 – Disable Auto App Updates

Developers are constantly working to improve their applications by updating content and adding new features. One of the best things about an online application store, like the Windows Store, is that you can easily keep your apps up to date. In fact, in Windows 8.1 these updates now happen automatically, but if you'd prefer to manually manage your app updates you can disable this setting.

Open the Windows Store and bring up the **Charms** menu, then select **Settings** and **App updates**. Then tap or click on the **Automatically update my apps** switch.

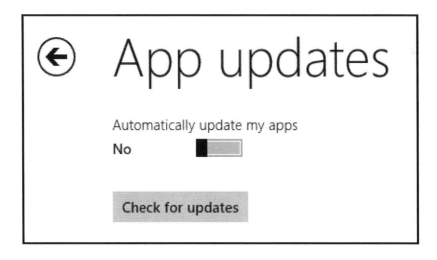

Tip # 96 – Clear Personal Info from Live Tiles

After a while the Live Tiles on your Start Screen can get filled with so much information that it's a bit of a mess, like a Desktop full of shortcuts, it's no longer helpful. To clear this info from your Live Tiles:

Touch – From the Start Screen, bring up the **Charms** menu and tap **Settings**. Select **Tiles** and tap the **Clear** button.

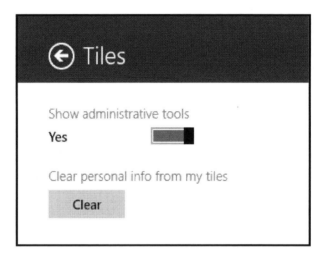

Key/Mouse – From the Start Screen, Press + **I** to go to Settings. Select **Tiles** and click the **Clear** button.

Tip # 97 – Managing App Space

If you find that you're running low on storage space you can check how much space is being taken up by individual apps.

Bring up the **Charms** menu, select **Search** and start typing "App sizes", then select it. Here you can identify any apps to remove from your system, select them and tap or click the **Uninstall** button.

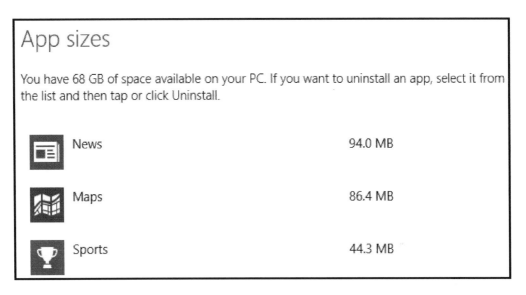

You can also uninstall Modern UI apps from the Start Screen or the Apps View by **long-pressing** or **right-clicking** on them to bring up the App bar and then selecting **Uninstall**.

Tip # 98 – Recover It

Windows 8 allows you to create a system recovery drive that can be used to restore Windows if your system ever crashes or becomes unstable.

To create a Recovery Drive, first close all open files and apps, go to the **Search Charm**, select **Settings** and start typing "recovery". Then tap or click on **Create a recovery drive**. Select **Yes** and **Next**, then connect a spare USB flash drive (Any existing data on the drive will be DELETED!). Select **Next** and tap or click on the **Create** button. When the recovery drive is ready, select **Finish**. Open **File Explorer** and select the drive in the navigation pane, then go to the **Drive Tools** contextual tab and **Eject** the drive. You should then label and store the Recovery Drive in a safe place.

Note: If you have a CD/DVD drive you will get the option to create an optical disc instead of a USB flash drive.

Tip # 99 – Refresh It

If your machine isn't running well, you can refresh Windows 8 without losing your Data. Apps that you installed from the Windows Store will be ok, but any apps installed from websites and discs will be deleted. To refresh your PC:

Touch – Bring up the **Search Charm**, select **Settings** and start typing "refresh". Then tap on **Refresh your PC without affecting your files** and follow the prompts.

Key/Mouse – Press 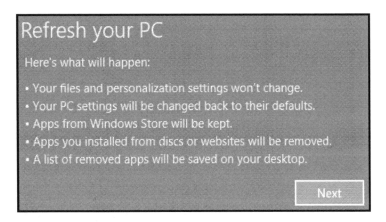 + **W** and start typing "refresh". Then click on **Refresh your PC without affecting your files** and follow the prompts.

Refresh your PC

Here's what will happen:

• Your files and personalization settings won't change.
• Your PC settings will be changed back to their defaults.
• Apps from Windows Store will be kept.
• Apps you installed from discs or websites will be removed.
• A list of removed apps will be saved on your desktop.

Next

Tip # 100 – Reset It

If you're giving your machine to someone else or you want to completely reinstall your PC then you can reset it back to its factory default settings. THIS WILL COMPLETELY REMOVE ALL YOUR DATA & APPS! So make sure that you have any important data backed up before you begin.

Touch – Bring up the **Search Charm**, select **Settings** and start typing "reset". Then tap on **Remove everything and reinstall Windows** and follow the prompts.

Key/Mouse – Press ⊞ + **W** and start typing "reset". Then click on **Remove everything and reinstall Windows** and follow the prompts.

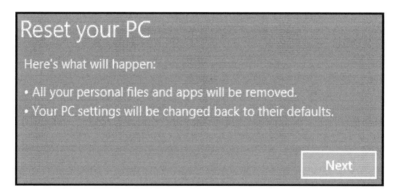

Chapter 10 – Keyboard Shortcuts

This chapter is a list of the most common Windows 8 Keyboard Shortcuts. Designed as a quick reference guide, the shortcuts have been split into the following categories: General, Accessibility, Charms menu, Desktop, Multiple Monitor, Power User and Semantic Zoom.

General shortcuts

⊞ **+ D** = Show Desktop

⊞ = Show Start Screen

Alt + Tab = Cycle between apps

⊞ **+ Tab** = Show recent apps

⊞ **+ Z** = Show App bars

⊞ **+ ,** = Peek at the Desktop

⊞ **+ . + Left Arrow** = Snap Modern apps or the Desktop to the left of the screen

⊞ **+ . + Right Arrow** = Snap Modern apps or the Desktop to the right of the screen

■ + . + **Down Arrow** = Close Modern apps or the Desktop

■ + **L** = Lock the screen

Ctrl + Alt + Arrow Keys = Rotate the screen

■ + **O** = Lock screen orientation

Ctrl + Alt + Del = Show the Windows Security screen

Accessibility shortcuts

■ + **U** = Ease of Access Center

■ + **Enter** = Narrator

Left Alt + Left Shift + PrtSc = High Contrast

Left Alt + Left Shift + NumLock = Mouse Keys

Hold Numlock for 5 seconds = Toggle Keys

Hold Right Shift for 8 seconds = Filter Keys

Press Shift 5 times = Sticky Keys

■ + **Plus Sign** = Start Magnifier and zoom in

■ + **Minus Sign** = Magnifier: zoom out

Ctrl + Alt + D = Magnifier: docked mode on Desktop

Ctrl + Alt + F = Magnifier: full screen mode

Ctrl + Alt + I = Magnifier: invert colors

Ctrl + Alt + L = Magnifier: lens mode

⊞ + **Esc** = Exit Magnifier

Charms menu shortcuts

⊞ + **C** = Show the Charms menu

⊞ + **Q** = Search Everywhere

⊞ + **W** = Search for Settings

⊞ + **F** = Search for Files

⊞ + **H** = Show Share charm

⊞ + **K** = Show Device charm

⊞ + **I** = Show Settings charm

Desktop shortcuts

■■ + **Left Arrow** = Snap the active window to the left of the screen

■■ + **Right Arrow** = Snap the active window to the right of the screen

■■ + **Up Arrow** = Maximize window

■■ + **Shift + Up Arrow** = Stretch window

■■ + **Down Arrow** = Minimize window

■■ + **M** = Minimize all windows

■■ + **Shift + M** = Restore all windows

■■ + **Home** = Minimize all windows except the active one and repeat to restore all windows.

■■ + **T** = Set focus on the Taskbar & cycle through running Desktop apps

■■ + **1** to **9** = Go to the app at the given position on the Taskbar

Ctrl + Mouse Wheel = Resize Desktop icons

Multiple Monitor shortcuts

⊞ + **P** = Projection options

⊞ + **Shift** + **Left Arrow** = Move active Desktop window to left monitor

⊞ + **Shift** + **Right Arrow** = Move active Desktop window to right monitor

Power User shortcuts

⊞ + **X** = Quick Link menu of advanced user commands

⊞ + **R** = Run command

⊞ + **Break** = System Properties

Ctrl + **Shift** + **Esc** = Task Manager

Alt + **F4** or **Alt** + **Fn** + **F4** = Close Desktop windows & Modern apps

Alt + **Up Arrow** = File Explorer: Go up one level in the directory structure

Alt = File Explorer: Use Ribbon KeyTips

Semantic Zoom shortcuts

Ctrl + Mouse Wheel = Semantic Zoom in Modern UI

Ctrl + Shift + Minus Sign = Zoom out

Ctrl + Shift + Plus Sign = Zoom in

Thanks for reading!

I hope you've learnt some useful tips that make using Windows 8 easier.

I'm always happy to hear your ideas, feedback and suggestions. Please send your emails to:

tim@tims-tips.com

For more great tips, please visit my website:

www.tims-tips.com

Regards, Tim Sievers.

33150550R00065